THE
POCKET
STREET ART

Published in 2025
by Gemini Gift Books
Part of Gemini Books Group

Based in Woodbridge and London

Marine House, Tide Mill Way,
Woodbridge, Suffolk IP12 1AP
United Kingdom

www.geminibooks.com

Cover illustration by Natalie Foss

ISBN 978-1-80247-309-4

Manufacturer's EU Representative: Eurolink Compliance Limited, 25 Herbert
Place, Dublin, D02 AY86, Republic of Ireland. admin@eurolink-europe.ie

Printed in China

10 9 8 7 6 5 4 3 2 1

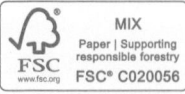

Picture credits: Alamy Stock Photo: ArtAngel: p88; Kingsley Davis: p62;
PA Images: p20; Sipa US: p26; Universal Images Group North America LLC:
p44. Freepik: p10–13,18–19, 23–5, 64, 68–9, 86–7, 99; JUICYFISH: p92, 94–5;
KJPARGETER: p6–7, 15–17, 22–3, 40; Macrovector: p4, 90–1, 93, 96–7, 99;
PIKISUPERSTAR: p91; Rawpixel: p4,14; REDGREY STOCK: p4, 28–9, 31–3, 108–9;
SERGEY KANDAKOV: p56–61; VectorCorp: p46–53. Getty Images: David
Corio: p54; Emanuele Cremaschi: p78; Eamonn M. McCormack/Stringer:
p100; Jack Mitchell: p34; Frédéric Soltan: p8; South China Morning Post: p70.

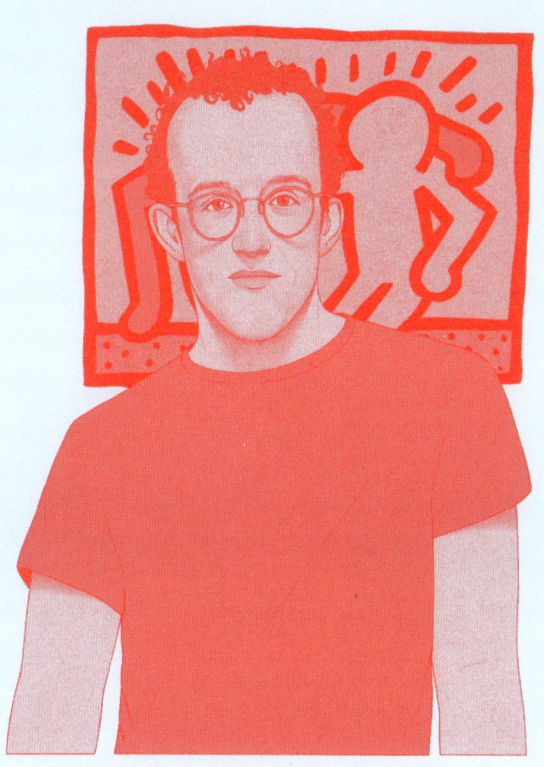

STREET ART

G:

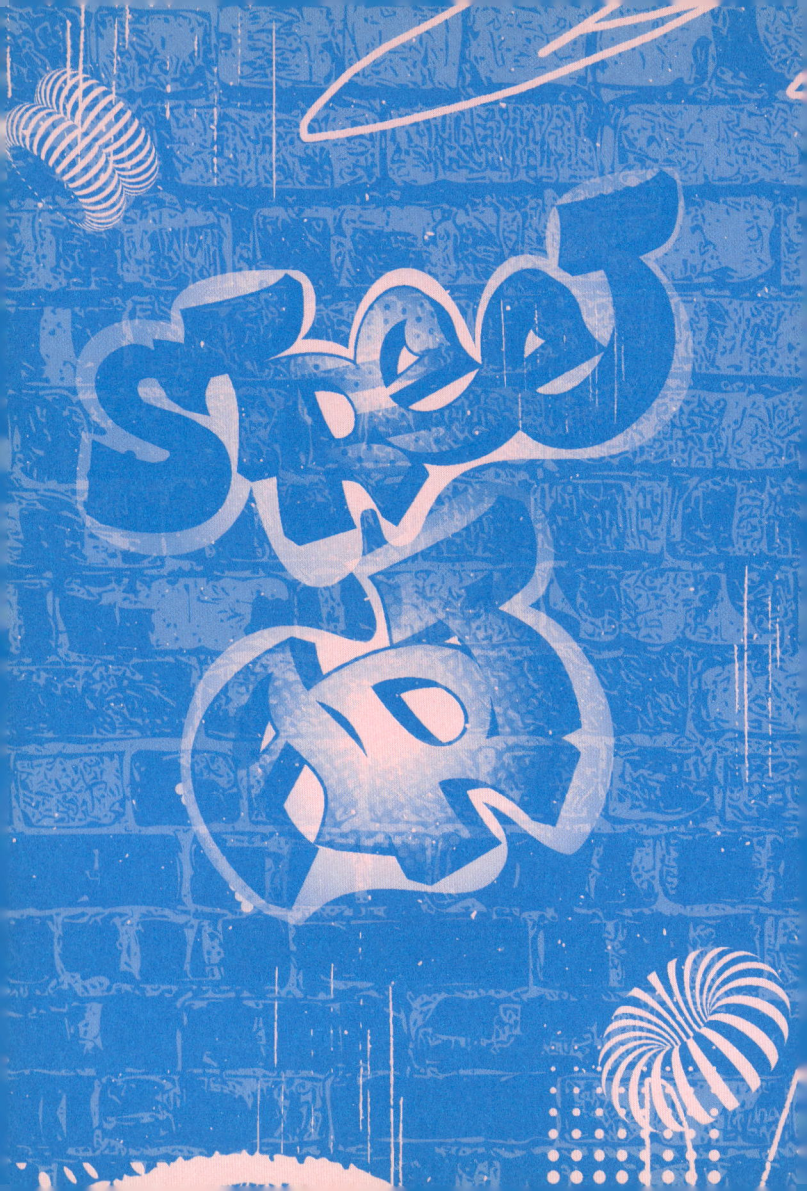

CONTENTS

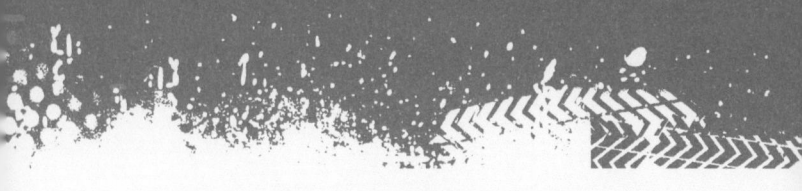

INTRODUCTION

Street Art is as old as the streets themselves. As long as humans have wandered around different places, they have left their mark. Evolving from graffiti, this provocative art form dates back to Roman times. But while simple graffiti has existed for centuries, these days Street Art is a recognized art form – and a big, colourful business.

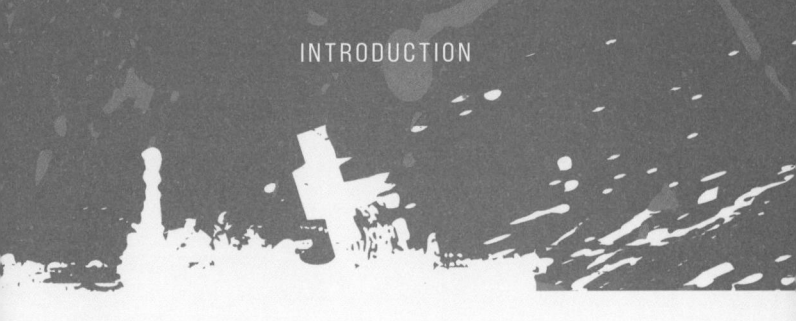

Ten artists have been chosen to demonstrate the breadth, excitement and sheer variety of Street Art for this book. Some of the most famous artists are included, such as Banksy, Keith Haring and KAWS, whose work adorns streets and buildings around the world, and often the walls of art galleries. While only a small selection is featured, all the artists bridge the gap between the underground and commercial in their own way, each making their indelible mark on this global cultural movement.

BUXTON ST. E.I.

বাক্সটন ষ্ট্রীট

SPITALFIELDS
CIT
FA

SIBOMANA

LEAVE THEM

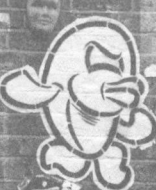

koez;

ORIGINS &
INFLUENCES

WHAT IS STREET ART?

In its most basic definition, Street Art is a visual art form that is made for public spaces. Encompassing a wide range of mediums and techniques, it blends artistic expression with social commentary. From graffiti, murals, stencils and stickers, to wheat-paste posters, installations and even performance art, it can almost be whatever you want it to be.

"Graffiti has been used to start revolutions, stop wars, and generally is the voice of people who aren't listened to."

BANKSY,
BANGING YOUR HEAD AGAINST A BRICK WALL, 2001

ORIGINS

The point of origin of Street Art as we know it today is undoubtedly the USA.

As early as the 1930s, subway carriages in the USA were hit with graffiti slogans and drawings. But from the 1960s, a distinctive new art movement emerged, alongside a new musical phenomenon: hip hop. Graffiti culture soon exploded, driven by the urban youth, and the artist's tag was key to claiming its space and voicing its identity.

By the 1980s, "graffiti art" was well
established. New creations freshly sprayed
on to the moving metal canvas of a
subway train rolled around New York
and other cities. This was rebellion, youth
and creativity combined. It was also –
unfortunately – illegal.

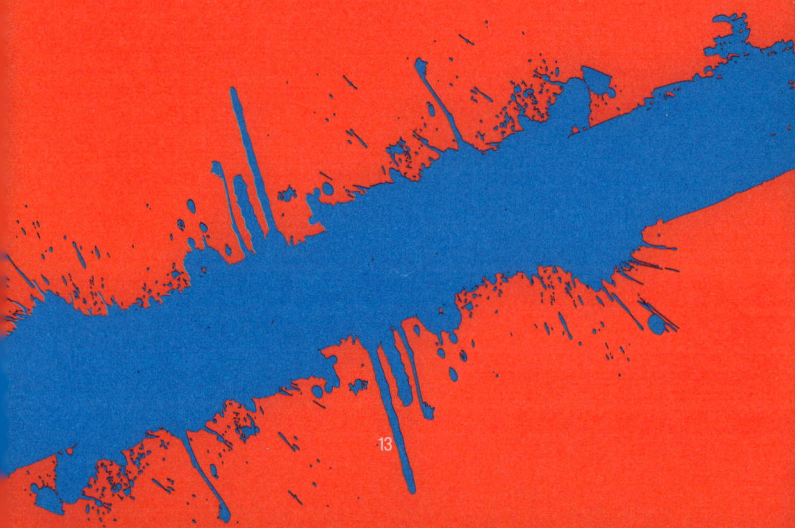

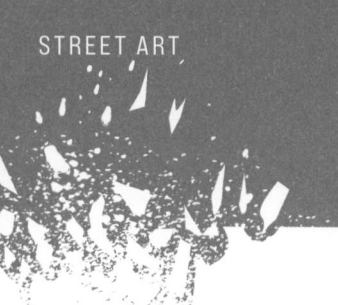

BREAKING THROUGH

As graffiti evolved into graffiti art, small slogans became huge "top-to-bottom", full-colour subway cars bearing the name of the artist. It was a movement with its own heroes, its own soundtrack, its own vocabulary. And it soon evolved further into Street Art.

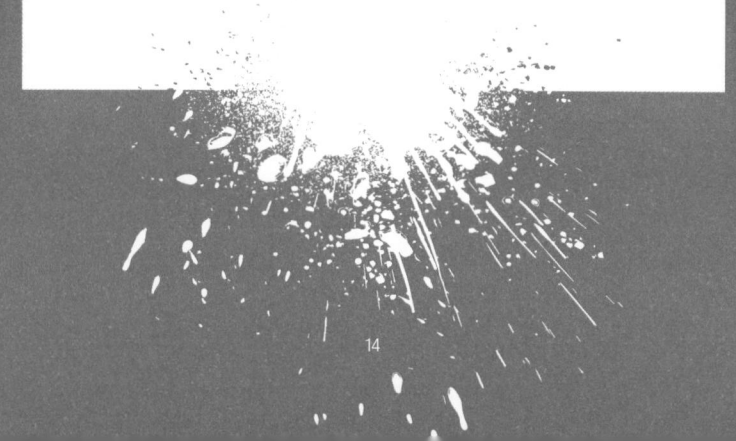

Using a wider array of techniques and messages, artists moved from street to studio. Keith Haring and Jean-Michel Basquiat (under his tag "SAMO") went from spray painting walls to exhibiting in renowned galleries around the world, blurring the lines between Street Art and high art, and commanding huge fees in the process.

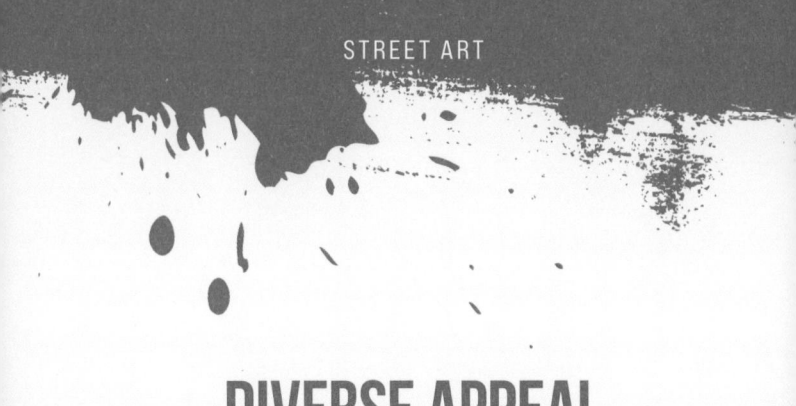

DIVERSE APPEAL

Today, most big cities feature amazing Street Art; some even have open-air "galleries" where artists can paint freely. The best Street Art is thoughtful, provocative and beautiful.

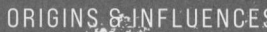

The medium of Street Art is incredibly diverse; it incorporates sculpture, drawing, stencilling and all sorts of creative endeavours. Relying on public accessibility, and ephemeral by nature, it is an art form that strives for individual expression mixed with cultural impact. The popularity of artists such as Banksy has driven its vast outreach and appeal.

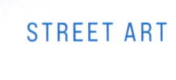

"Nothing is important... so everything is important."

**KEITH HARING,
CANVAS.SAATCHIART.COM, 2017**

EVOLUTION

While still retaining its rebellious roots, Street Art today has certainly entered mainstream culture. Showcased at festivals and through dedicated tours, its commercialization is not always welcome.

However, while discussions about its authenticity have often surfaced, its ability to raise pertinent questions still rings true today. With activism at its core, but now with a wider reach, how will this dynamic and creative movement evolve? Well, one can only watch this space.

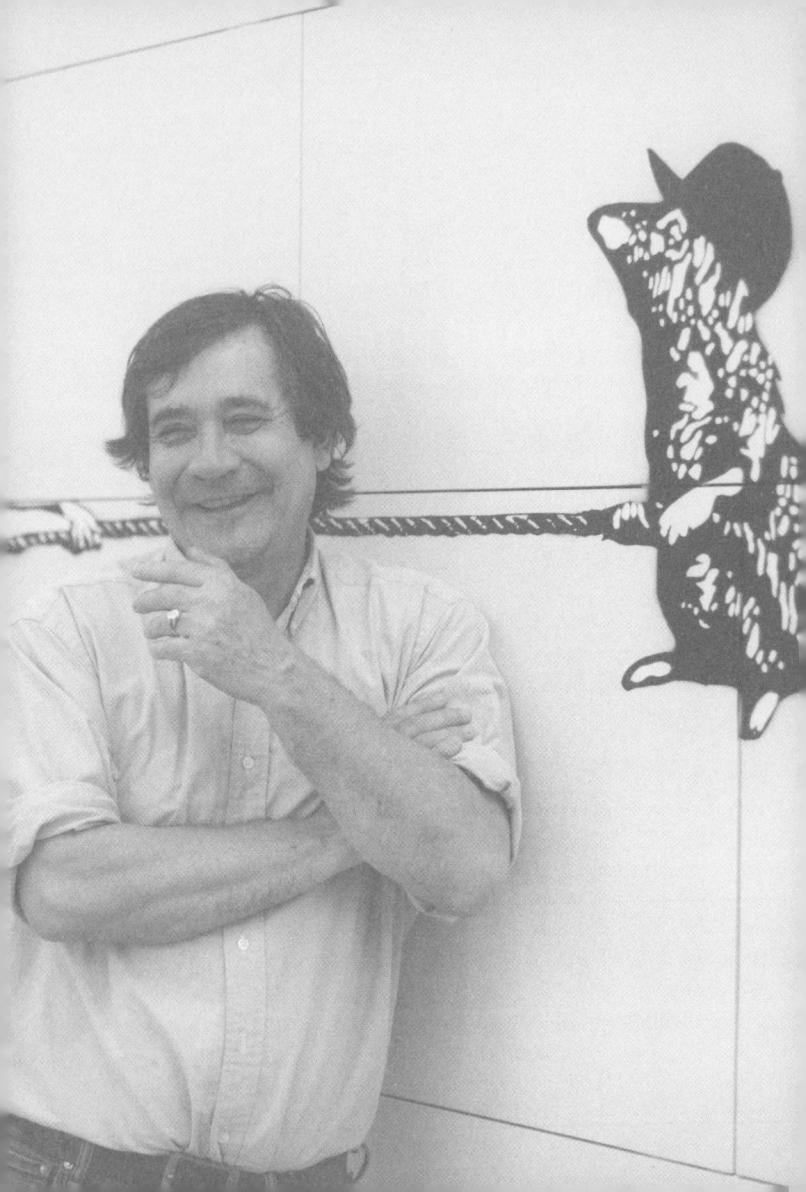

BLEK LE RAT

1951–

Place of birth:

Paris, France

Key works:

Rats (1980s)
Rope Pulling (1983)
Man Who Walks Through Walls (2007)
Ballerina (2011)

EARLY YEARS

Blek le Rat is a French Street Artist whose real name is Xavier Prou. One of the elder statesmen of graffiti art, he is described by many as the father of stencil graffiti art in particular. He started working around Paris in the early 1980s, after studying at the École des Beaux-Arts in Paris. Rats are common in his work, but he also makes reference to classic artists, such as Caravaggio, Michelangelo and Leonardo da Vinci.

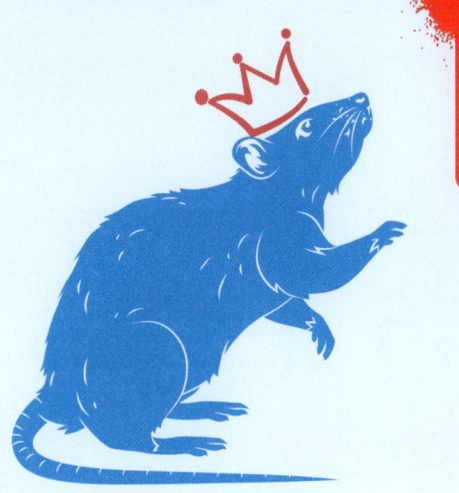

Blek le Rat has been a big influence on many other artists, Banksy in particular, who once stated, "Every time I think I've painted something slightly original, I find out that Blek le Rat has done it as well, only twenty years earlier."

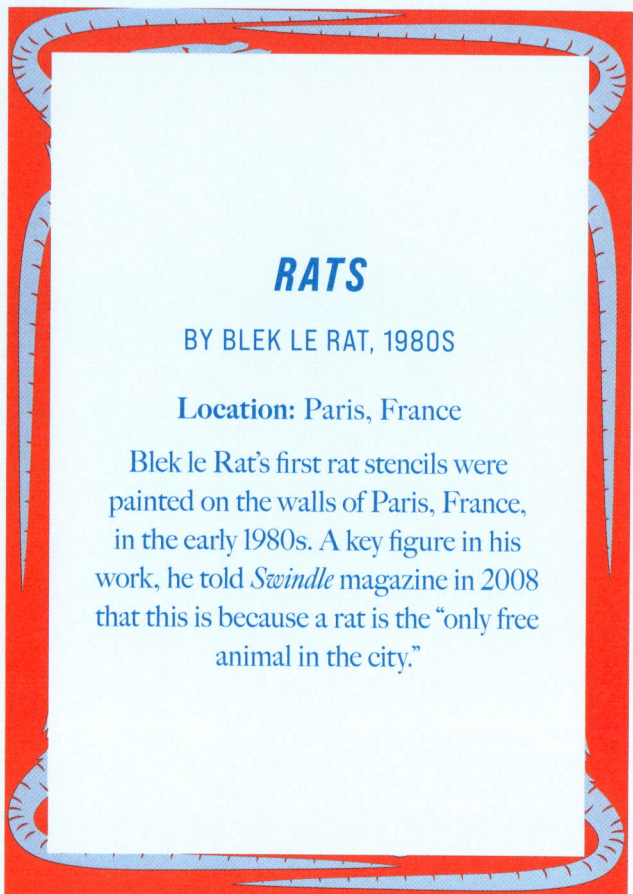

RATS

BY BLEK LE RAT, 1980S

Location: Paris, France

Blek le Rat's first rat stencils were painted on the walls of Paris, France, in the early 1980s. A key figure in his work, he told *Swindle* magazine in 2008 that this is because a rat is the "only free animal in the city."

"When I was twenty years [old] in 1972 I took a trip to New York City, and that's where I first discovered graffiti."

BLEK LE RAT,
INTERVIEW WITH MATTHEW ELLER,
STREETARTNEWS.NET, 2022

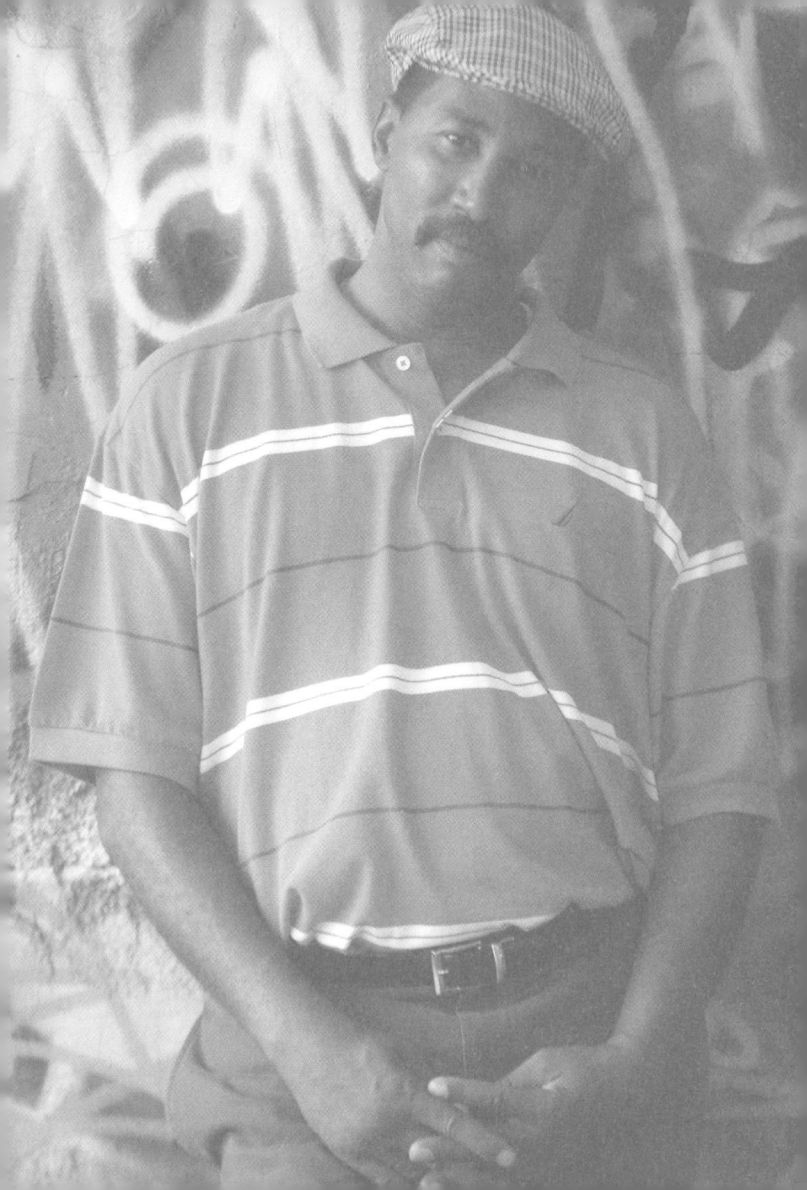

CORNBREAD

1953–

Place of birth:

Philadelphia, USA

Key works:

Tagging the Jackson 5's tour jet (1967)
Cornbread Loves Cynthia (1970s)
Cornbread Lives (1971)

EARLY YEARS

Darryl McCray, known as "Cornbread", is often credited with being the first modern graffiti artist. His colourful, vivid designs and messages helped take graffiti art – often associated with vandalism and gang activity – into the mainstream.

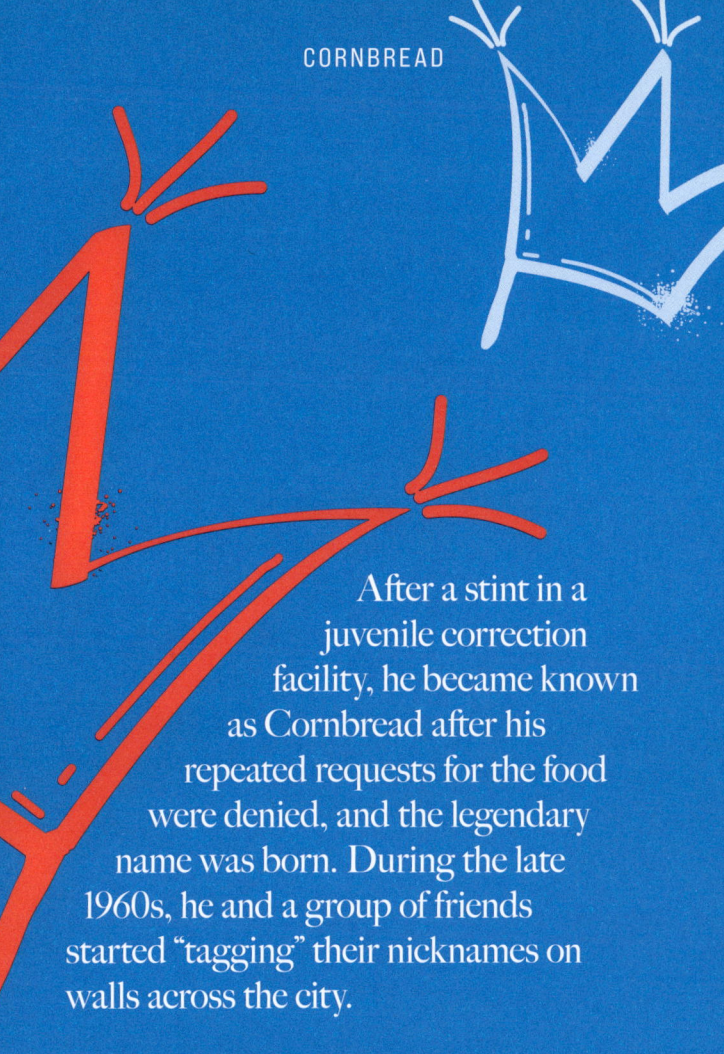

After a stint in a
juvenile correction
facility, he became known
as Cornbread after his
repeated requests for the food
were denied, and the legendary
name was born. During the late
1960s, he and a group of friends
started "tagging" their nicknames on
walls across the city.

GRAFFITI TAGS

Cornbread is remembered mostly for a few key campaigns. In *Cornbread Loves Cynthia*, he wrote this declaration of love for a girl in his class everywhere along their route home. But it was writing his name on the Jackson 5 jet that brought him recognition; following the band's trip to Philadelphia, his tag made the news when their plane landed back in California.

CORNBREAD LIVES

BY CORNBREAD, 1971

Location: Elephant at the Philadelphia Zoo, USA

On reading in a Philadelphia newspaper that he had been killed as a result of a gang-related shooting, Cornbread famously tagged an elephant (with water-based paint) at the Philadelphia Zoo, clearly stating that "Cornbread Lives". Street artist Bansky has since known to have carried out similar acts more recently, inspired by the renowned event.

THE TAG LIVES ON

McCray has since been the subject
of exhibitions and a documentary.
He is now a public speaker
and youth advocate who gives
motivational talks about his days
as a tagger, his run-ins with the law
and his struggles with drugs.

"The hip hop and graffiti cultures were both born and bred in Philadelphia. Anything in New York gets magnified because it is the media capital of the world. But, New York did not start hip hop."

CORNBREAD,
WORCESTER MAGAZINE, 2018

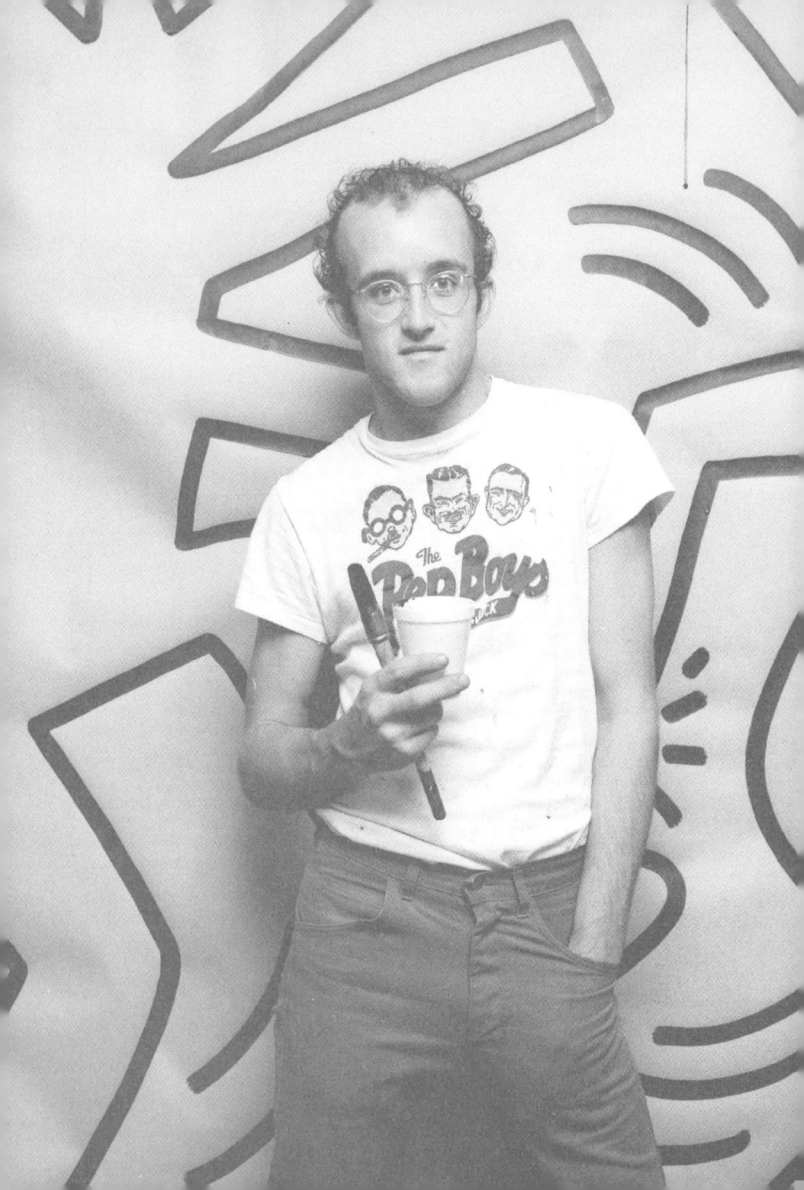

KEITH HARING

1958–1990

Place of birth/death:

Pennsylvania, USA/New York, USA

Key works:

Keith Haring Mural (1984)
Statue of Liberty (1986)
Crack is Wack (1986)
Berlin Wall Mural (1986)
Tuttomondo (1989)

EARLY YEARS

Keith Haring was inspired by the popular culture and animations that surrounded him, such as Dr. Seuss and Walt Disney. He began to develop his own artistic skills as he learned cartooning techniques from his father.

He moved to New York City in 1978 – after dropping out of art school – and enrolled in the School of Visual Arts. At the time, the art scene was thriving. Art was everywhere: in the streets, the subway and in the clubs.

"The trains in 1978 and 1979 were incredible. That's when an artist would spend eight hours on one car."

KEITH HARING,
INTERVIEW MAGAZINE, 1984

"I didn't start doing graffiti until two years after I got to New York. Jean-Michel Basquiat was one of my main inspirations for doing graffiti."

KEITH HARING,
INTERVIEW MAGAZINE, 1984

EARLY SUCCESS

From 1980 to 1985, Haring created many artworks in the New York City subway. As he gained recognition, he also began to participate in numerous group and solo exhibitions, and soon his reputation grew on an international scale.

In April 1986, Haring opened the Pop Shop, selling T-shirts, posters and toys with his designs on them. He wanted people to have access to his work but at a low cost.

CRACK IS WACK

BY KEITH HARING, 1986

Location: Harlem, New York, USA

Crack is Wack is a mural that overlooks New York's FDR Drive. Haring was famously ordered to cover it up, only for the New York City Parks Department to later commission a new mural on the same theme as a warning against crack cocaine use, which was rampant across the major cities of the United States in the late 1980s.

HARING STYLE

Haring's work was featured in over a hundred solo and group exhibitions, and he collaborated with artists as diverse as Madonna, Grace Jones, William Burroughs, Timothy Leary, Yoko Ono and Andy Warhol. He has also completed many public projects, designed sets and backdrops for theatres and clubs, and painted murals all over the world.

His style is instantly recognizable. He made use of the universal concepts of birth, death, love, sex and war, which resonated with a large audience and ensured his popularity to this day.

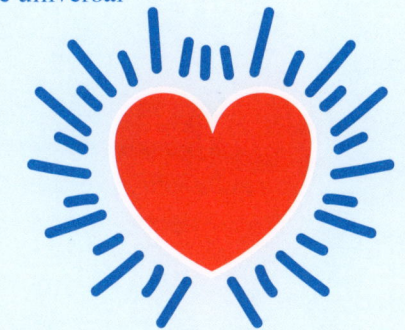

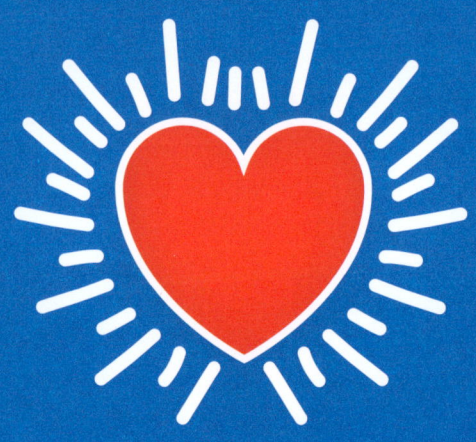

CHARITY WORK

Between 1982 and 1989, Haring produced more than 50 public artworks in cities around the world, for charities, hospitals and orphanages.

He was diagnosed with AIDS in 1988. In 1989, he established the Keith Haring Foundation, to provide funding and imagery to AIDS organizations and children's programs. He frequently spoke about his own illness to raise awareness about AIDS. He died at the age of 31 on 16 February 1990.

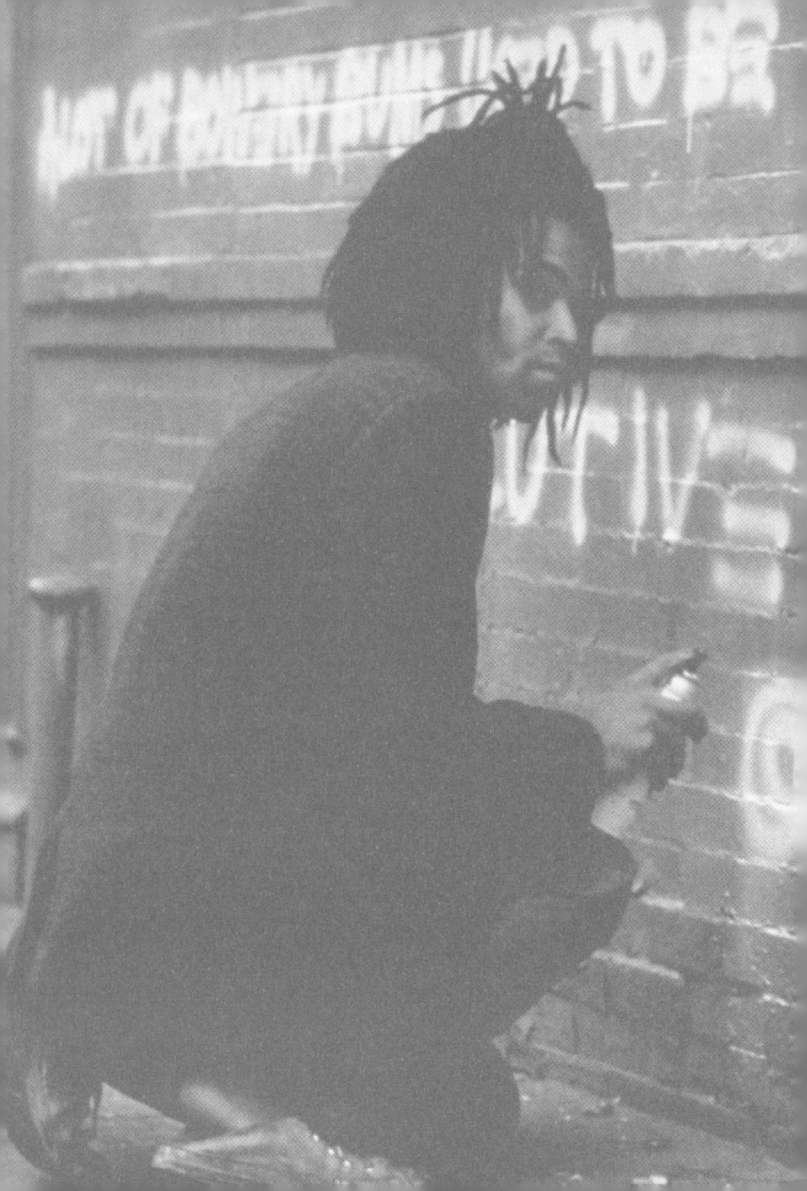

JEAN-MICHEL BASQUIAT (SAMO)

1960–1988

Place of birth/death:

New York, USA/New York, USA

Key works:

SAMO© (1978–80)
Untitled (LA Painting) (1982)
Ten Punching Bags (Last Supper) (1985–6)

EARLY YEARS

Jean-Michel Basquiat was born in Brooklyn, New York, on 22 December 1960. His father was Haitian-American and his mother Puerto Rican. This diverse cultural heritage is omnipresent in his work, and he helped bring both cultures into the often elitist art world.

Basquiat was self-taught. He began drawing at an early age, and his mother always encouraged him to pursue his artistic talents.

"I never went to an art school. I just looked at a lot of things."

JEAN-MICHEL BASQUIAT,
DOWNTOWN 81, 2000

SAMO

Basquiat first attracted attention for his graffiti in New York City in the late 1970s. His tag was "SAMO", and he often placed cryptic messages on subway trains and Manhattan buildings. In his early work, he was known for using a crown motif, to represent Black people as royalty and saints.

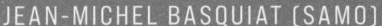

In 1977, Basquiat quit
high school, a year before
graduation. To make ends
meet, he started selling
sweatshirts and postcards
featuring his artwork on the
streets of New York.

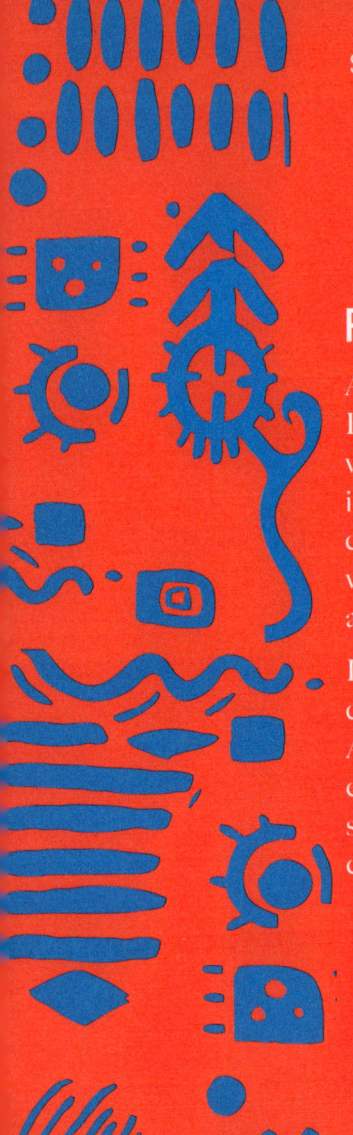

PAINTING

After struggling for three years, Basquiat found fame in 1980 when his work was featured in a group show. He received critical acclaim for its fusion of words, symbols, stick figures and animals.

In the mid-1980s, Basquiat collaborated with the artist Andy Warhol. The work they exhibited together featured a series of corporate logos and cartoon characters.

UNTITLED (LA PAINTING)

BY JEAN-MICHEL BASQUIAT, 1982

Location: Private collection

This painting depicts a skull, composed of black brushstrokes with red, yellow and white rivulets against a blue background. In May 2017, a Japanese billionaire bought *Untitled* for $110.5 million (£85 million) at auction. The sale set records for the highest price for a work by an American artist, by Basquiat and by a Black artist.

FAME AND DEATH

After the exhibition with Warhol, Basquiat continued to exhibit successfully. But as his popularity increased, so did his personal problems. He died of a drug overdose on 12 August 1988 – he was 27 years old.

"I don't think about art while I work, I try to think about life."

JEAN-MICHEL BASQUIAT,
INTERVIEW WITH ISABELLE GRAW,
ARTSY.NET, 1986

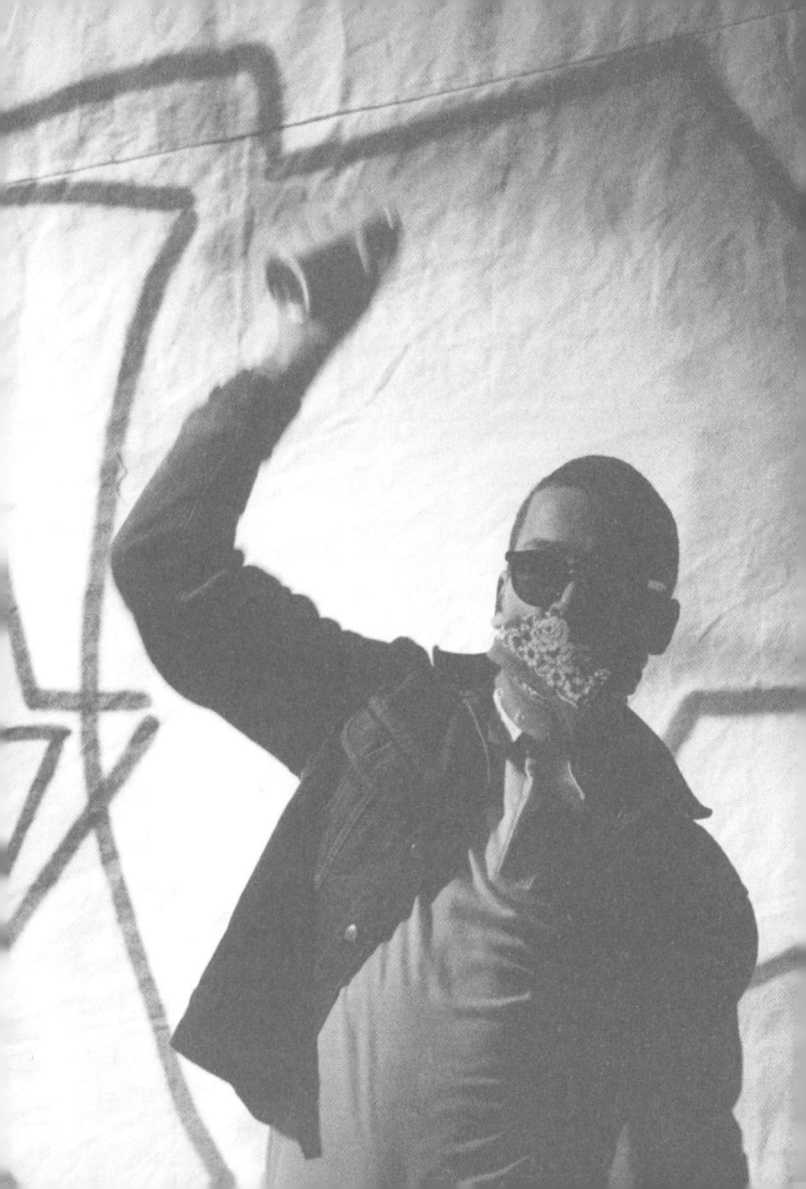

DONDI WHITE

1961–1998

Place of birth/death:

New York, USA/New York, USA

Key works:

New York subway trains, various
Children of the Grave, Parts 1–3 (1978–80)
Born Again (1986)
SM General Notes (1989)
Rain Proof Dance (1992/2007)

EARLY YEARS

Donald "Dondi" Joseph White was an American graffiti artist born in 1961. One of five brothers, his parents were of African-American and Italian-American origin. He used various nicknames for tagging his art, but Dondi was his favourite and derived from a childhood nickname.

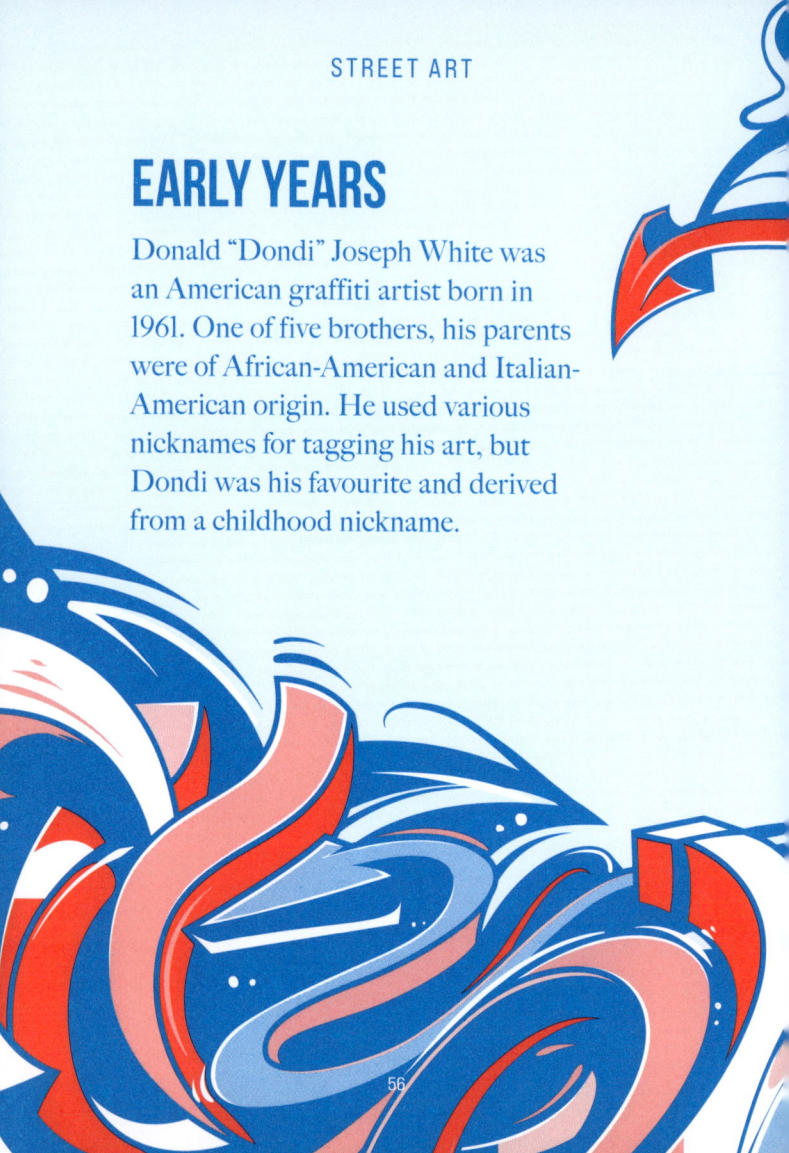

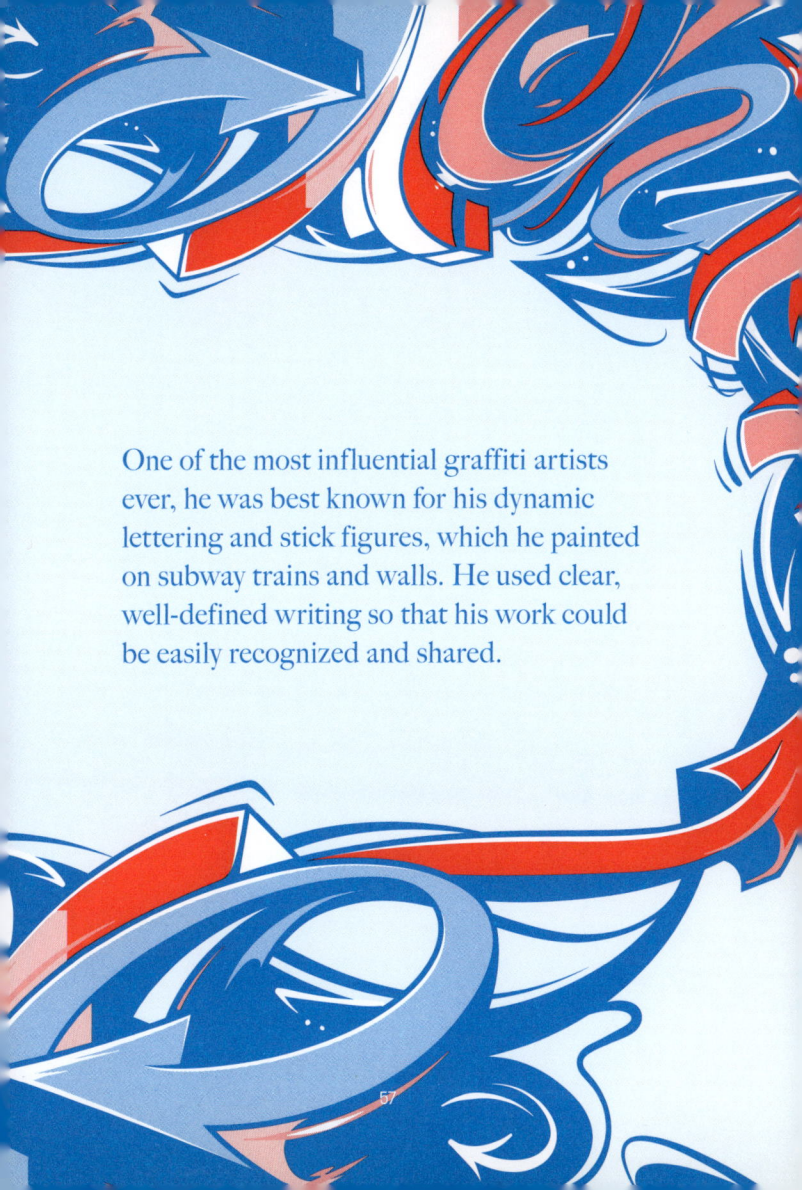

One of the most influential graffiti artists ever, he was best known for his dynamic lettering and stick figures, which he painted on subway trains and walls. He used clear, well-defined writing so that his work could be easily recognized and shared.

GROUP TACTICS

Dondi began his career in the early 1970s as part of the group of graffiti artists known as The Odd Partners, working on the New York City subways. In 1977, Dondi formed his own group, known as CIA (Crazy Inside Artists), and established his reputation as one of the most stylistically innovative and influential graffiti artists of his generation.

CHILDREN OF THE GRAVE, PARTS 1–3

BY DONDI WHITE, 1978–80

Location: New York City Subway train, USA

Dondi's most iconic artwork was created when he painted over three whole cars on the New York City Subway. Parts 2 and 3 were documented in a film by photographer Martha Cooper. Taking the title of a Black Sabbath song, it was an unlikely choice at a time when graffiti art was mostly associated with hip hop.

FROM TAG TO CANVAS

After years of tagging, Dondi successfully made a transition from graffiti to gallery, and he turned his hand to canvas, rubbing shoulders with other graffiti creators such as Keith Haring and Jean-Michel Basquiat. He died on 2 October 1998. Decades after his death, he still influences and inspires many artists.

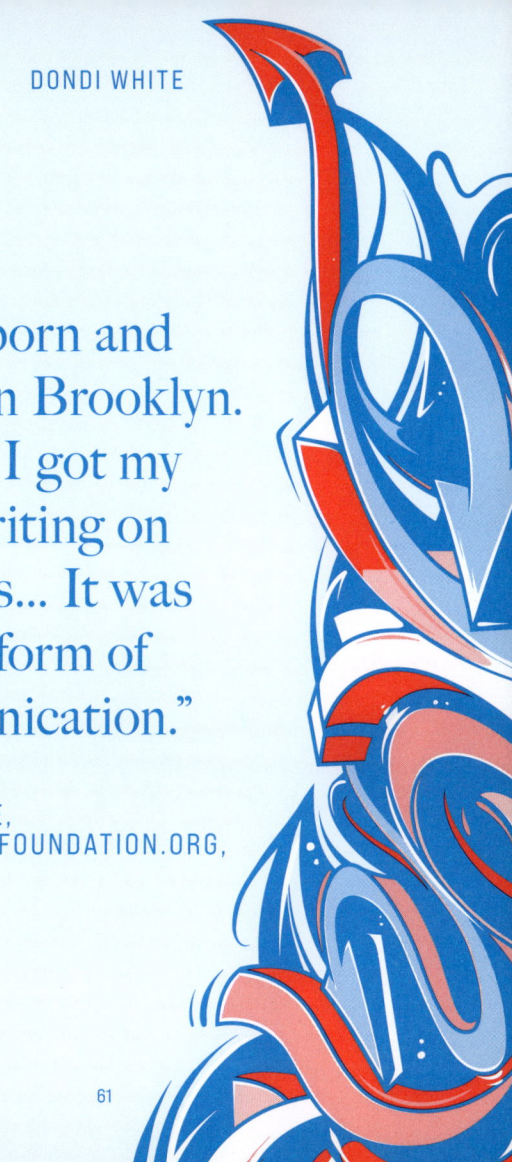

"I was born and raised in Brooklyn. I guess I got my start writing on subways... It was a good form of communication."

DONDI WHITE,
DONDIWHITEFOUNDATION.ORG,
1990

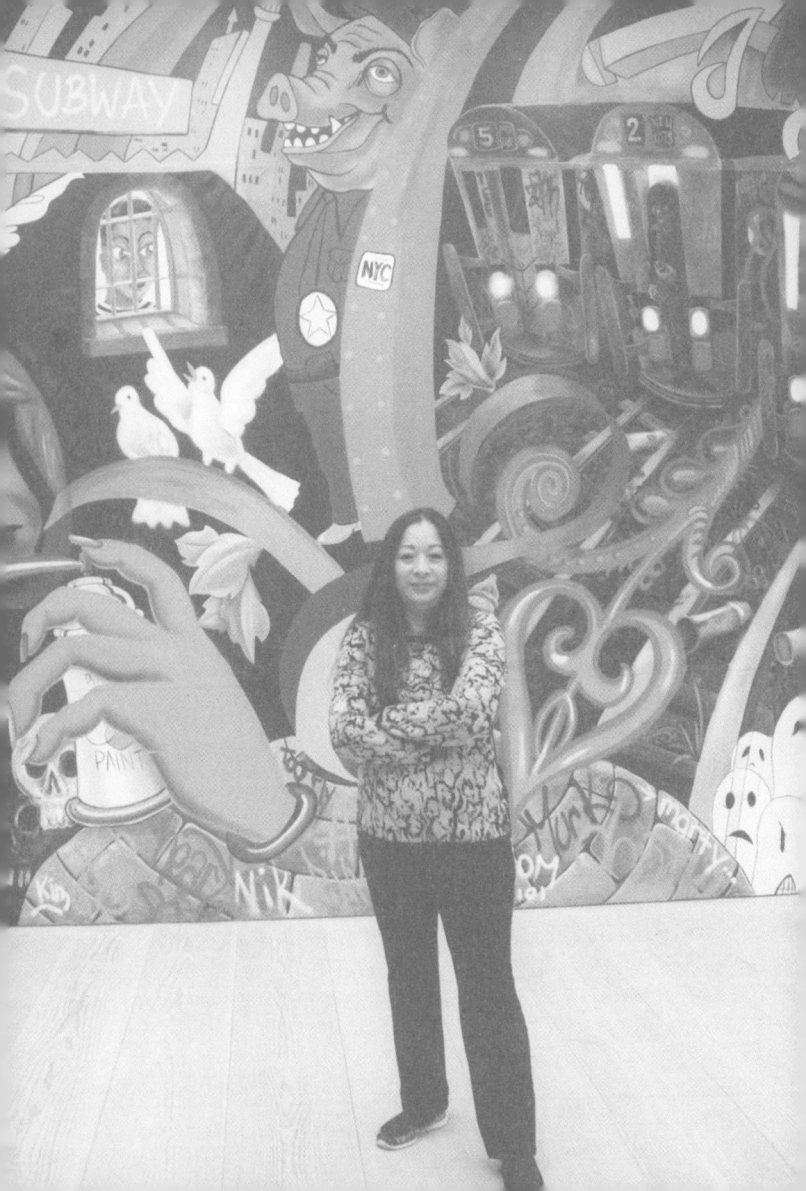

LADY PINK

1964–

Place of birth:

Ambato, Ecuador

Key works:

New York subway trains, various (1979–85)
Pink Piece (1980)
Butterfly in a Bubble (1981)
Brick Woman (2000)
Series of murals in collaboration with
Jenny Holzer (2023)

EARLY YEARS

Lady Pink was born in Ecuador in 1964 and raised in New York City. She started her graffiti career in 1979 and was one of the first women active in the early 1980s subculture.

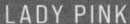

Lady Pink chose her name because she loved historical romances and she wanted people to know she was a woman. She used graffiti and murals as acts of rebellion and self-expression, and to empower women.

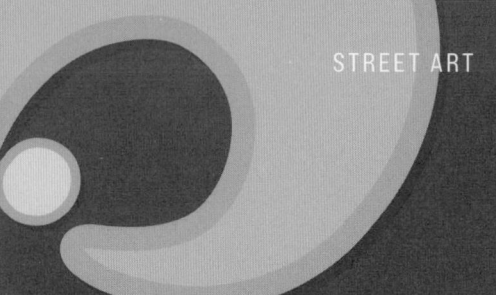

WILD SIDE

Lady Pink is considered a cult figure in the hip-hop subculture since the release of the movie *Wild Style* in 1982, in which she had a starring role.

PINK

BY LADY PINK, 1983

Location: C train, New York City Subway, USA

This classic signature piece is the epitome of Lady Pink's style in the early graffiti days of her work. Painting the train from top to bottom in full pink colour, it is a theme she used with variation in other similar works on the New York Subway at the time, and for which she gained a cult following.

MOVING ON

Lady Pink's paintings have entered many important art collections, such as those of the Whitney Museum, the MET in New York City, the Brooklyn Museum, the Museum of Fine Art in Boston and MoMA. She also established herself in the fashion world, collaborating with brands such as Louis Vuitton, Supreme and Lancôme.

Today, Lady Pink continues to create new paintings. She also holds mural workshops for teens and lectures college students across the world.

"I haven't done illegal graffiti in decades. But fine, you want to call me a street artist? Graffiti artist? A hip-hop icon? A feminist? Whatever."

LADY PINK,
INTERVIEW WITH ROGER GASTMAN,
BEYONDTHESTREETS.COM, 2021

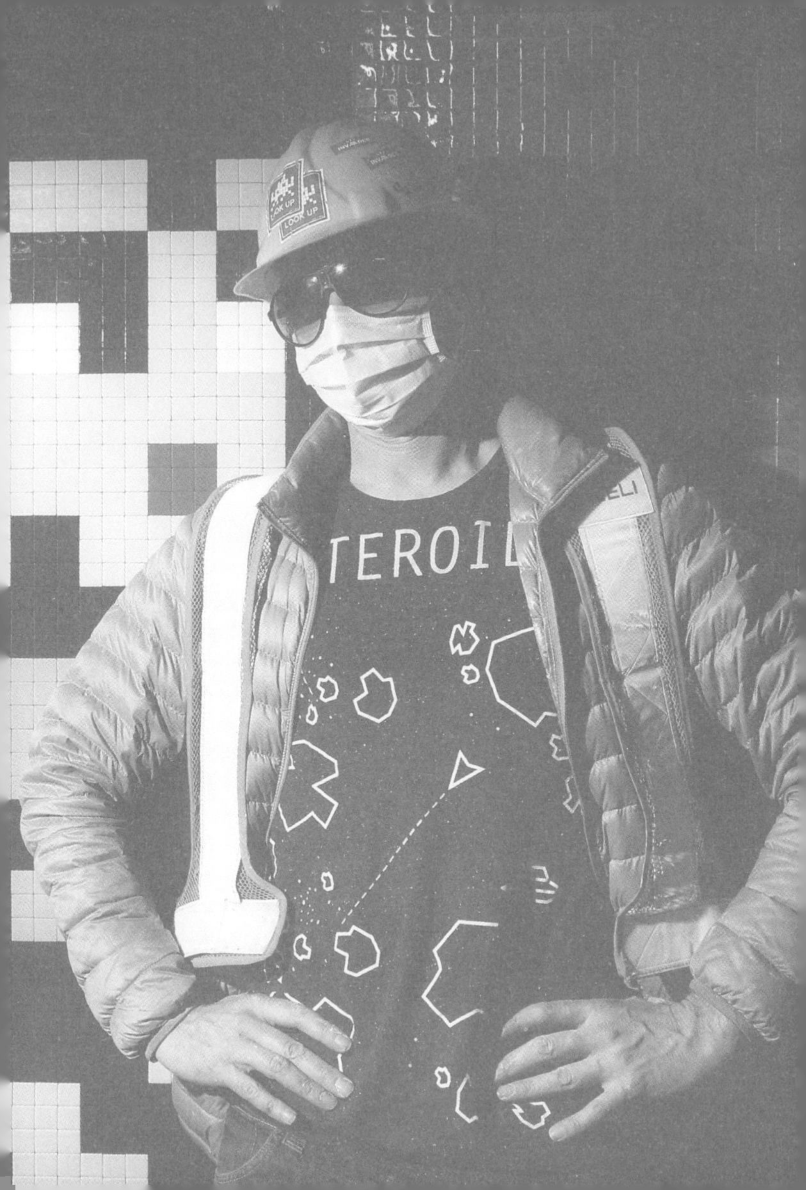
LOOK UP
TEROI

INVADER

1969–

Place of birth:

Paris, France

Key works:

PA_004 (1998)
PA_1431 (2019)
"Rubikcubism" series (since 2005)
Rubik Mona Lisa (2005)

EARLY YEARS

Born Franck Slama, Invader is a French street artist. He came to fame through his tile mosaics, many of which resembled "space invaders" from the 1970s video game. His style is much imitated and very distinct, modelled on the pixelated art of video game culture and 1980s popular culture.

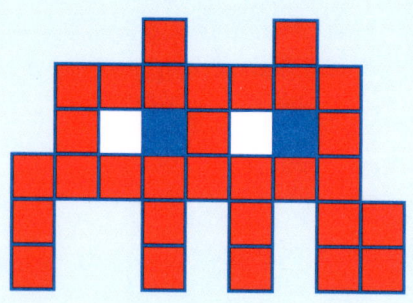

PA_1431

BY INVADER, 2019

Location: The Eiffel Tower, Paris, France

Invader installed one of his works at the top of the Eiffel Tower in 2019. This piece featured a small cloud alongside his usual figure. It's an artwork that is difficult to see from the ground, and is only visible to those visiting the tower.

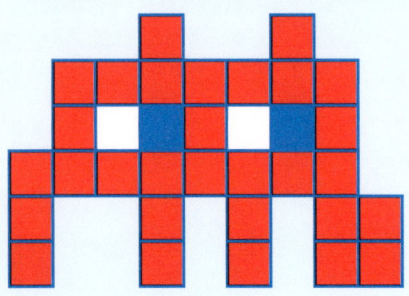

ENVIRONMENTAL HACKER

Always working in secret to conceal as much of his identity as possible, his mission from the beginning has been to invade public spaces with art.

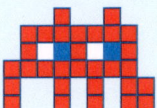

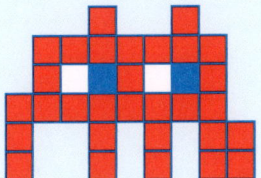

Since 1998, Invader has put up over 4,000 tile-based mosaics in over 80 cities around the world. He has named this ongoing artistic endeavour his "Space Invaders" project. He has even managed to send his work into space, with the help of astronaut Samantha Cristoforetti in 2019.

BEYOND REACH

Many of Invader's Street Art mosaics have been stolen, causing him to place them in ever-more-inaccessible places, and sometimes even to seek permission to install them. Many buildings have been known to rise in value once adorned with one of his recognizable pieces.

Early in the twenty-first century, Invader created a series of works named "Rubikcubism", where he used Rubik's Cubes to create large images. Some have commanded high prices in sale rooms.

"It's like a bank robbery. I know exactly how everything needs to go."

INVADER,
THE NEW YORKER, 2023

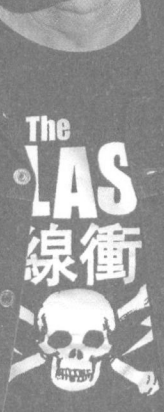

SHEPARD FAIREY

1970–

Place of birth:

South Carolina, USA

Key works:

André the Giant Has a Posse (1989)
OBEY clothing and art line (2001)
Hope (2008)
Purple Project (2014)
Make Art Not War (2014)

EARLY YEARS

Shepard Fairey is an American muralist and graphic artist whose work combines Street Art activism with an entrepreneurial spirit. As a teenager, Fairey had an interest in skateboard culture. By 1984, he was designing and selling hand-decorated boards and T-shirts. After graduating from Rhode Island School of Design in 1992, he quickly gained national attention.

ANDRÉ THE GIANT HAS A POSSE

BY SHEPARD FAIREY, 1989

André the Giant Has a Posse was a sticker campaign featuring the wrestler André René Roussimoff (André the Giant) and the word "Obey". It was the start of a series that helped push Fairey into the spotlight, selling more than one million copies. In an interview with Kobi Annobil in *Format* magazine in 2008, Fairey has since referred to its much more humble beginnings, stating, "The André the Giant sticker was just a spontaneous, happy accident."

HOPE

In 2008, Fairey found mainstream success with the red and blue *Hope* poster, which was adopted by the Barack Obama presidential campaign, featuring the then candidate in red, white and blue.

Fairey often uses art for political purpose. He protested the Iraq War, supported Occupy Wall Street, and has advocated gun control, anti-racism and environmental protection.

"Being in the streets, whether it's an art piece like a huge mural that I would do, or a street art piece that's a rebellious act of intervention... these are really important things to demonstrate a commitment."

SHEPARD FAIREY,
RED·EYE MAGAZINE, 2004

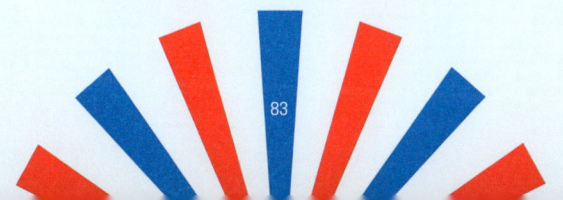

83

"I have spent
my entire life
building credibility
for my artistic voice."

SHEPARD FAIREY,
RED·EYE MAGAZINE, 2004

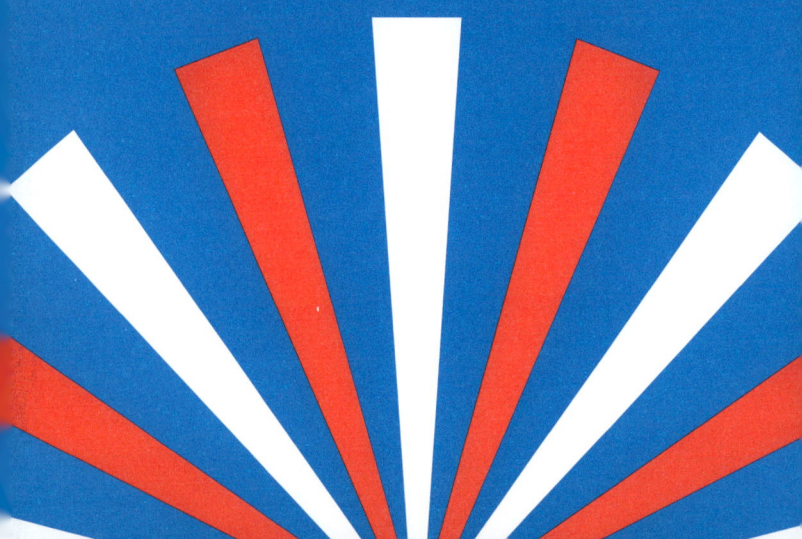

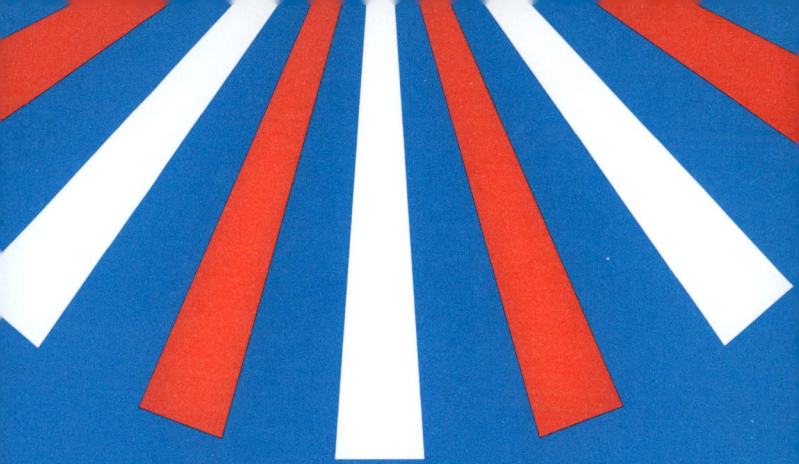

MURALS

Fairey is also famous for his murals, which include the *Peace Elephant* (2011) in Los Angeles and the *Purple Project* (2014) in Johannesburg, honouring Nelson Mandela.

Later murals call attention to some of the major issues facing the United States in the late 2010s and early 2020s: prison (*The Stamp of Incarceration* in Philadelphia, 2015), immigration (*American Dreamers* in Los Angeles, 2018) and voting restrictions (*Voting Rights Are Human Rights* in Milwaukee, 2020).

COMMERCIAL SUCCESS

The Institute of
Contemporary Art, Boston,
hosted Fairey's first major solo
exhibition, Supply and Demand,
in 2009. Fairey's artwork is
included in the collections of the
Smithsonian in Washington, D.C.,
the Los Angeles County Museum
of Art, and the Victoria and
Albert Museum in London.

"It's been nice to see a lot of people who came to my work through street art now getting more sophisticated in looking at the fine art world too."

SHEPARD FAIREY,
INTERVIEW MAGAZINE, 2019

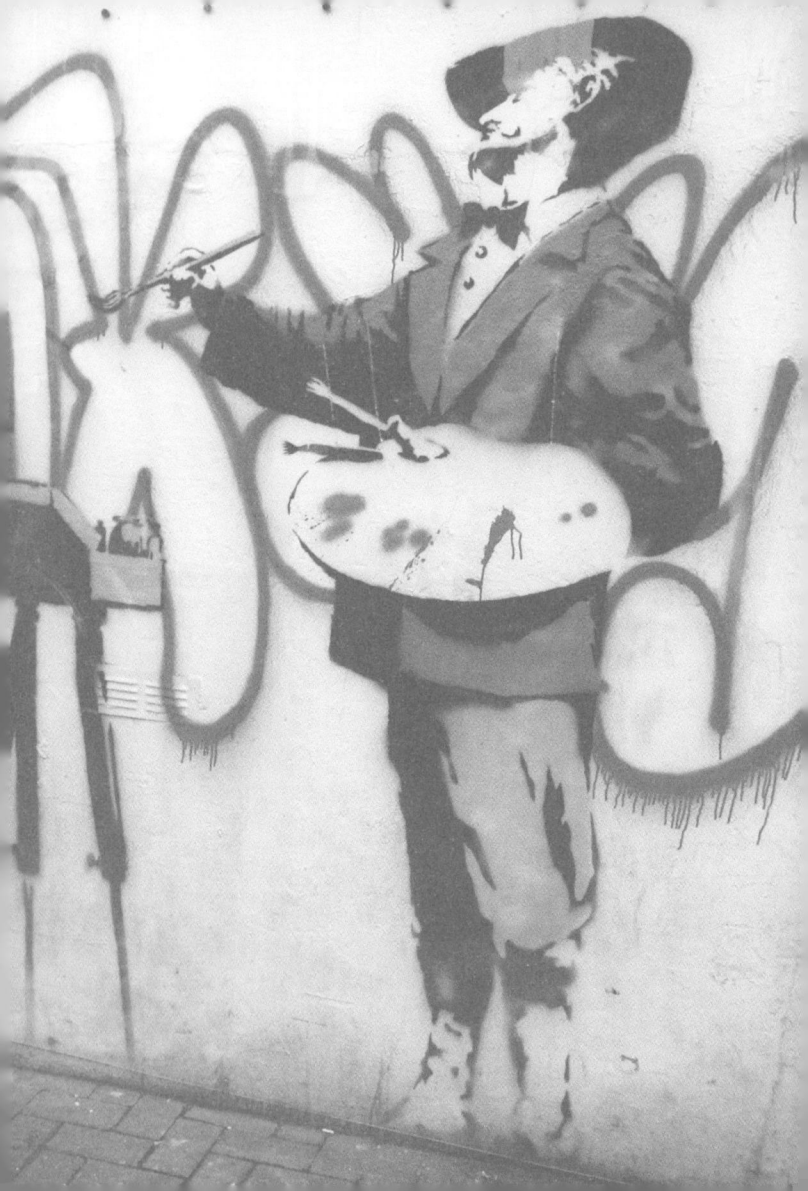

BANKSY

1974–

Place of birth:
Bristol, UK

Key works:
Girl with Balloon (2002)
Laugh Now (2002)
Love is in the Air (2003)
Kissing Coppers (2004)
Naked Man Hanging From Window (2006)

EARLY YEARS

Banksy is an anonymous British artist known for his highly political art, often created in public places, which usually appears unexpectedly. He started as a freehand graffiti artist in 1993, and his work grew out of the underground Bristol scene.

Banksy began to use stencils in 2000, as he needed to work quickly – traditional graffiti took him too long. He merged graffiti art with installation and performance.

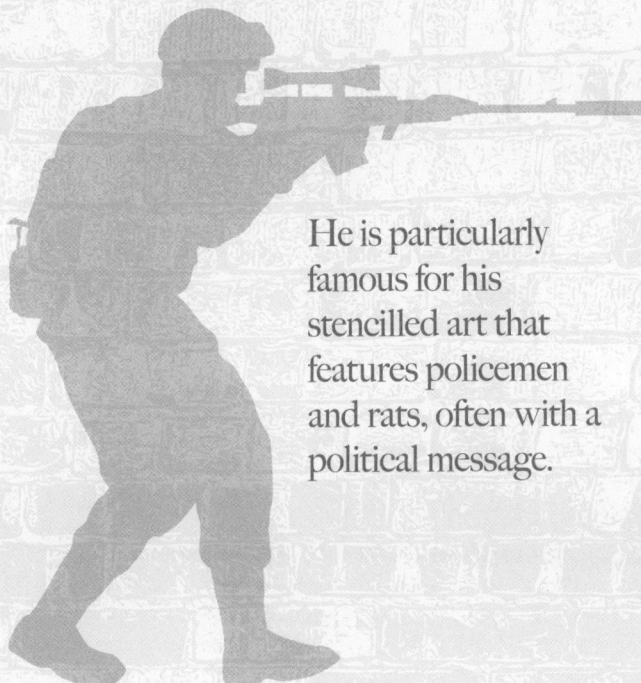

He is particularly famous for his stencilled art that features policemen and rats, often with a political message.

STREETS AHEAD

Banksy's identity is a closely-guarded secret, and the subject of much speculation. However, he still managed to be the subject of a documentary film, *Exit Through the Gift Shop*, in 2010 and puts on multiple exhibitions.

His influence on the Street Art scene is immense, so much so that a new phase, "the Banksy effect", was coined to show his influence.

"Go out! Trash things! Have fun!"

BANKSY,
INTERVIEW WITH NIGEL WRENCH,
BBC, 2003

DIVIDED STATES

In 2017, *The Walled Off Hotel* opened in Bethlehem. Constructed next to the wall that separates Israel from the Palestinian territories, the hotel boasted "the worst view of any hotel in the world" and contained a gallery exhibiting work by Palestinian artists.

LOVE IS IN THE AIR

BY BANKSY, 2003

Location: West Bank Wall

Perhaps one of Banksy's most powerful pieces, its original placement was on the West Bank Wall that separates the city of Jerusalem from Palestinian neighbourhoods. Also known as "Flower Thrower", the stencil depicts a man masking his face with a bandana as he prepares to throw a bunch of flowers like one would throw a grenade or molotov cocktail, symbolizing the power of love and peace over conflict. The work is incredibly famous and prints were soon released, followed by T-shirts, phone covers and more.

HAVING FUN?

In the 2003 exhibition Turf War, Banksy painted on the bodies of live pigs.

During his Crude Oils exhibition in London in 2005 he released 200 live rats into the gallery.

In September 2015, Banksy opened the temporary amusement park Dismaland in Weston-super-Mare, England. He described it as a "family attraction that acknowledges inequality and impending catastrophe."

INFAMOUS

Banksy is the most famous graffiti artist in the world. His work generates huge media and public attention and his style is instantly recognizable. He has managed to remain anonymous and rarely gives interviews – when he does he usually conducts them via e-mail or on tape with his voice altered.

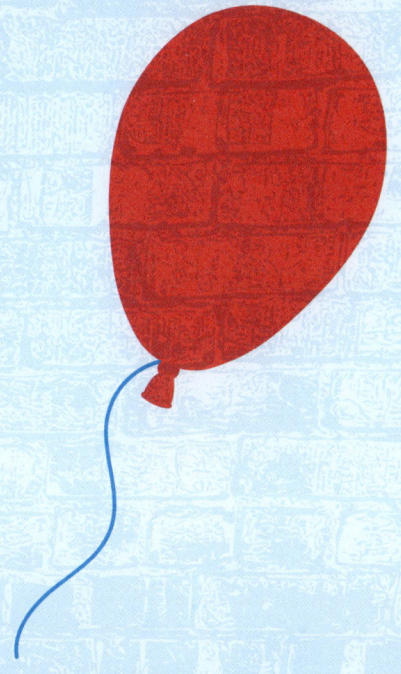

Banksy remains committed to Street Art. He once said that life in a city in which graffiti was legal would be "like a party where everyone was invited."

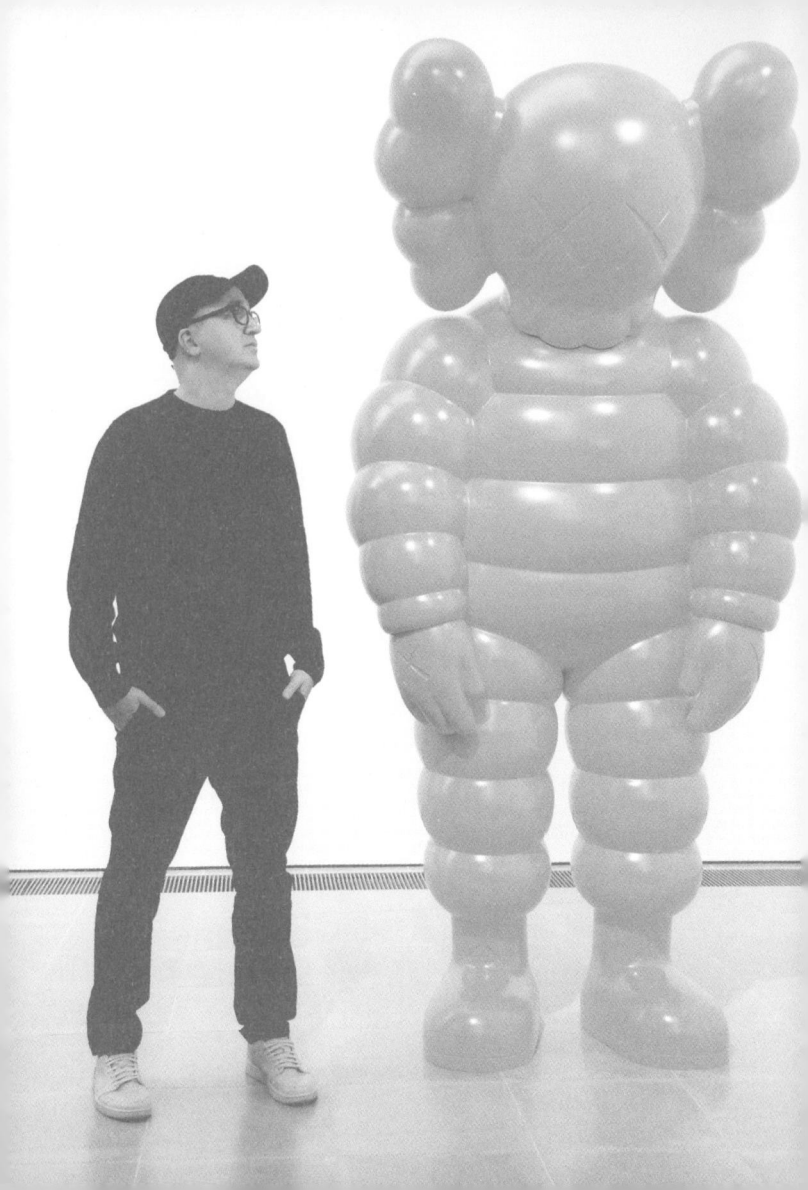

KAWS

1974–

Place of birth:

New Jersey, USA

Key works:

Companion (1999)
Untitled (Kimpsons) 2001
Accomplice (2001)
The KAWS Album (2005)

EARLY YEARS

Artist Brian Donnelly goes by the name of KAWS. He was originally a graffiti artist and his work includes repeated use of figurative characters and motifs. His style is famous worldwide, merging street culture, pop icons and fine art.

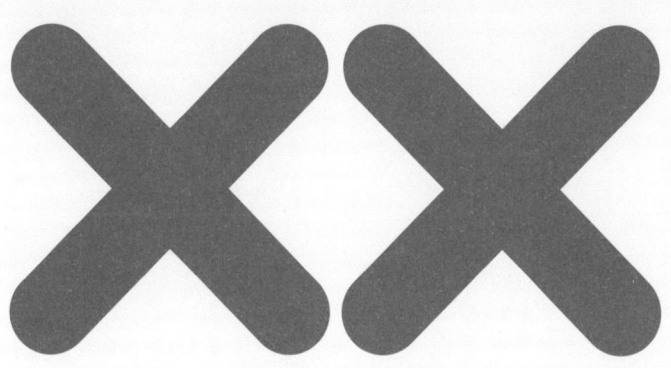

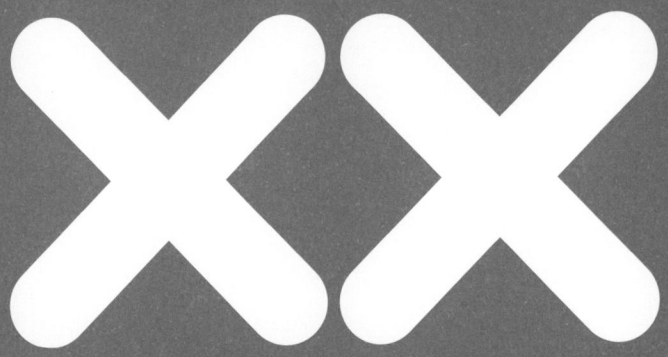

KAWS attended the School of Visual Arts in New York City. After he moved on from graffiti, he began to work in paint and sculpture and is now more famous for his acrylic statue work.

COMMERCIAL SUCCESS

Today, KAWS' work is popular, and sells at many price points, from $50 (£40) to over $1 million (£800,000). His sculptures range in size and are made from various materials, including fibreglass, aluminum, wood, bronze and steel.

His work is exhibited in galleries and museums, held in the permanent collections of public institutions and avidly collected by individuals. *The Kaws Album* (2005) sold for around $15 million (£12 million).

COMPANION

BY KAWS, 1999

Location: Various

Companion is a grayscale clown-like figure based on Mickey Mouse, with his face obscured by both hands and two bones sticking out of his head. In 1999, the Japanese toy company Bounty Hunter produced and sold a vinyl *Companion* toy. The figure has since been further adapted into many different mediums, including sculptures for exhibitions.

COLLABORATIONS

KAWS has collaborated with many companies, including A Bathing Ape (clothing), Bounty Hunter (toys) and Medicom Toy (toys). In 2016, he entered into an ongoing relationship with clothing store Uniqlo to produce a line of affordable T-shirts and accessories.

KAWS lives and works in Brooklyn, New York.

"Graffiti was great because it helped me learn about kids all over the world, that there really was this community unlike any that exists, even now, in contemporary art."

KAWS,
INTERVIEW WITH EVAN PRICCO,
JUXTAPOZ.COM, 2018

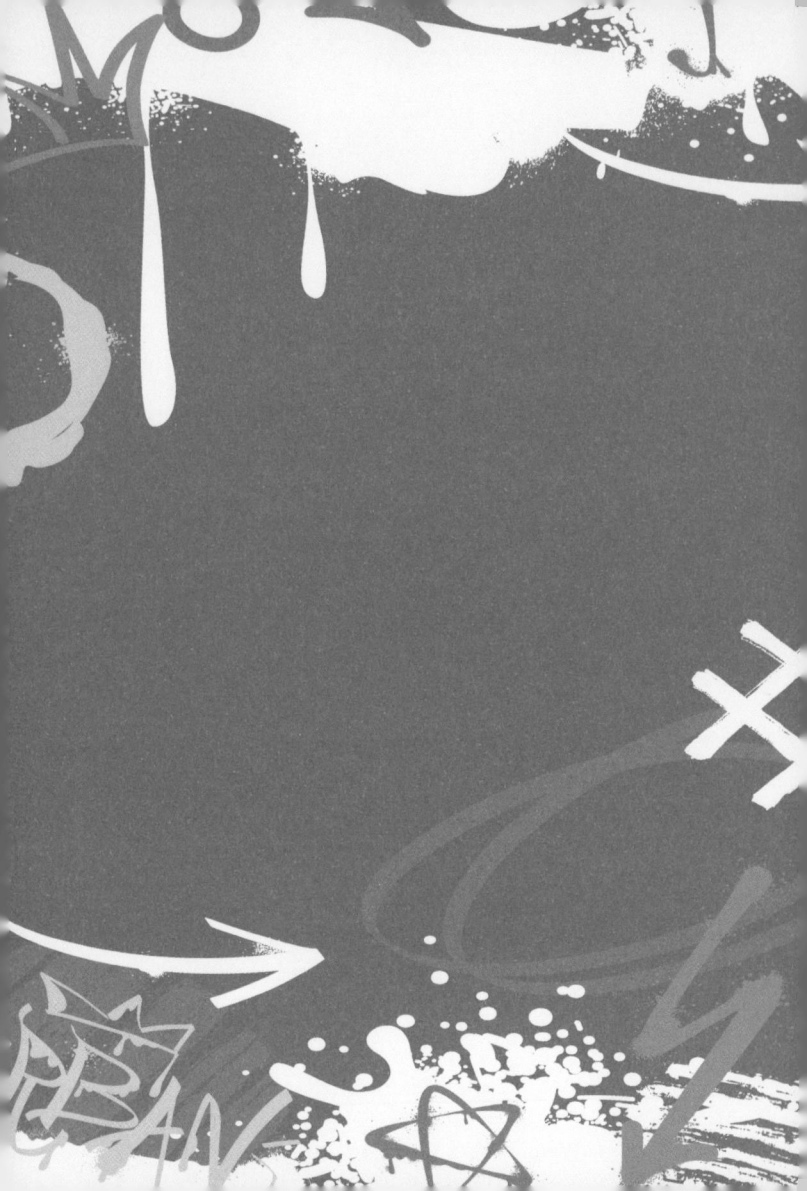

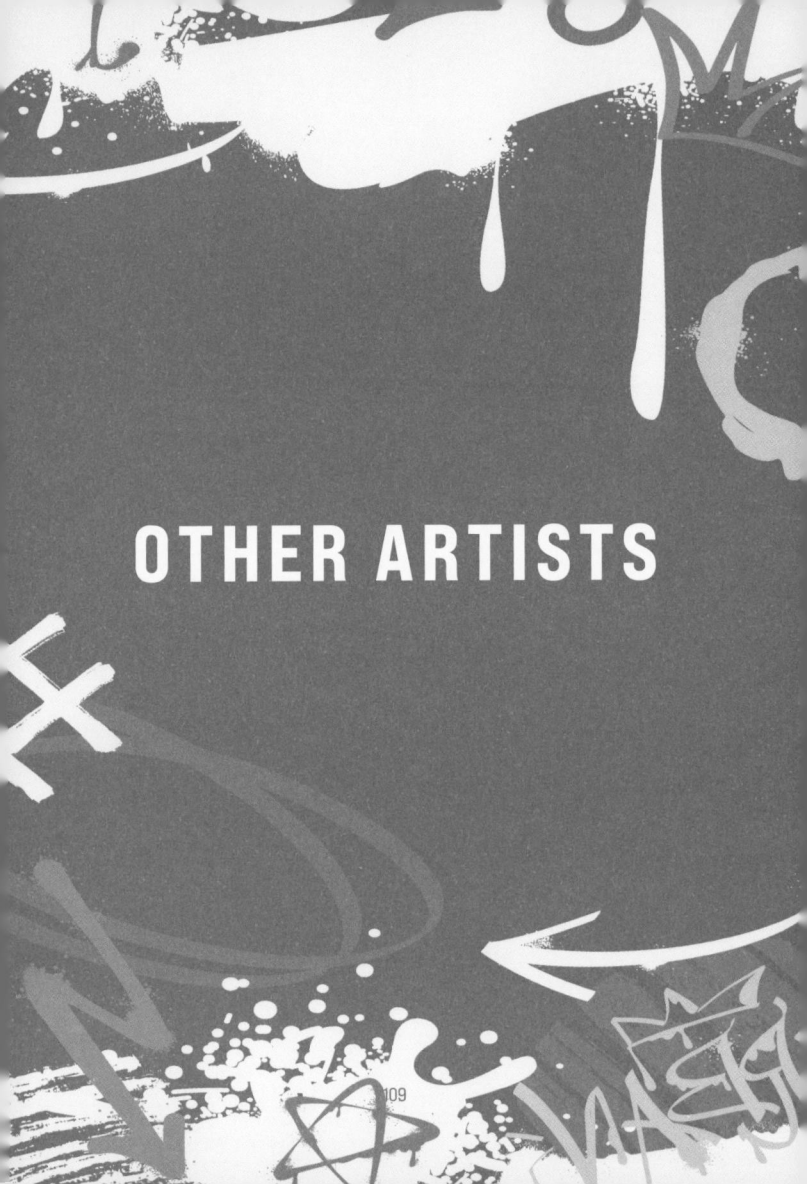

OTHER ARTISTS

TAKI 183

TAKI 183 was the "tag" of a Greek-American graffiti artist named Demetrius (1953/4–) who was active during the late 1960s and early 1970s in New York City. He started writing his name after seeing someone else's signature on the walls of his neighbourhood. He chose "TAKI" – a diminutive for a Greek name – and his street number. He first wrote his name around Washington Heights (where he lived), then in Midtown Manhattan (where he went to school), and eventually in the Upper West Side (where he worked).

After the *New York Times* published an article in 1971 with the headline "'TAKI 183' Spawns Pen Pals", his legend grew. He was even rumoured to have tagged a Secret Service car and the Statue of Liberty.

"The father of modern day graffiti."

STREETARTNYC.ORG, 2015

FUTURA 2000

Leonard Hilton McGurr (1955–), otherwise known as FUTURA 2000, began painting New York subways in the late 1970s. In 1980 he painted an iconic whole car, entitled *Break*. He was one of the first graffiti artists to be shown in contemporary art galleries in the early 1980s, alongside artists such as Keith Haring and Jean-Michel Basquiat.

In 1988, FUTURA 2000 illustrated the sleeve for The Clash's single 'This is Radio Clash'. He accompanied the band on their Combat Rock tour, spray painting in the background while they played. By the 1990s, he had taken advantage of the expansion of street culture and collaborated with brands such as Supreme, Nike and BMW, fashion labels Comme des Garçons and Louis Vuitton, as well as with Japanese artist Takashi Murakami.

"The pursuit of something that people equate to success? Which is usually material objects and some sort of a monetary status? It's not my thing."

FUTURA 2000,
INTERVIEW WITH CHRISTIAN BARKER,
JOURNEYSINARTISTRY.COM, 2023

BLADE

Steven Ogburn (1957–), known as "BLADE", was born in the Bronx, New York. His nickname was simply "The King of Graffiti". He first did graffiti in 1972, and painted more than five thousand subway trains in his career.

His famous *Mainstreams* painting was created on canvas in 1990 as a response to other artists moving away from traditional graffiti style. He exhibited his first works on canvas in a European art show in 1981, and participated in many individual and collective shows in notable venues, such as the Whitney Museum of American Art, New York, the Museum of Contemporary Art (MOCA), Los Angeles and the Groninger Museum in the Netherlands.

"BLADE
is not just any
well-known artist;
he is the greatest
of the great."

GUILLERMO DE LOUW,
UNFRAMED-ART-GALLERY.COM, 2024

OS GEMEOS

Os Gemeos (1974–) are street artist twin brothers Gustavo and Otavio Pandolfo from São Paulo, Brazil. One inspiration of theirs was the video of 'Buffalo Gals', the 1982 song by Malcolm McLaren and the World's Famous Supreme Team, which featured Dondi White spray painting. They are famous for graffiti art as well as murals.

The brothers' style is very recognizable: big murals with bold colours (lots of yellow and red) and often a humorous element. They sometimes include optical illusions. You can see their work all over the world, from India to Brazil and from London to Hong Kong.

"We became real addicts of hip-hop – we learned how to dance, how to DJ, how to rap, and how to spray."

OS GEMEOS,
ARTINTHESTREETS.ORG

ROA

ROA (1976–) is a "traditional" street artist, painting large, intricate murals in open spaces. He most commonly makes images of animals, and they are usually in black and white, although he sometimes uses bright splashes of colour. Originally from Belgium, he has painted all around the world.

Some of his key works include a large crane on the side of a building in Brick Lane, London (2010) and various animals, including an anteater and an armadillo, occupying the entire height of a condo in East Harlem, New York (2015).

"I think a mural
is always a
combination, like
almost a duet,
between the mural
and whatever you
paint it on, and the
architecture of the
wall itself."

ROA,
INTERVIEW WITH MATTHEW ELLER,
STREETARTNEWS.NET, 2022

FAITH47

Faith47 (1979–) is mostly based in South Africa, but she travels extensively and her artwork can be found in more than 50 cities around the world. She started in graffiti art in 1997 and has since become a multidisciplinary artist, working with drawing, sculpture, video, soft arts, and, of course, her huge, colourful murals.

Recurring themes in her artwork are female empowerment, questioning of authority, and environmental and humanitarian issues. Her art is often political in nature, challenging and encouraging change. Many have evocative names, for example *The Taming of the Beasts* (Shanghai, 2012), *The Psychic Power of Animals* (New York City, ongoing), *Landfill Meditation* (South Africa, 2015) and *The Freedom Charter* (South Africa, 2010).

"I didn't study in the traditional manner – all of my education has been through practical experience and my own independent investigation."

FAITH47,
STREET ART (LONELY PLANET), 2017

RETNA

Retna (Marquis Lewis, 1979–) is an American graffiti artist who also produces fine art. He worked with graffiti from a young age, and is part of the AWR/ Mad Society Kings crew, a Los Angeles graffiti collective.

His fine art comprises fascinating letterforms and decorative typography, including calligraphy from ancient and lesser-known scripts. It is instantly recognizable and his use of colour is very original, often painting text in white over coloured or textured backgrounds. His work is seen on the cover of Justin Bieber's album *Purpose* (2015).

"As a kid, I was looking at these things on the freeway, these really colourful paintings, and I wanted to do it."

RETNA,
"ART IN THE STREETS",
MOCA.TV, EP. 6, 2012

ALICE PASQUINI

Alice Pasquini (1980–) has a distinctive, colourful style that is immediately recognizable. She has painted all around Europe and much of the rest of the world, including Brazil, Canada and the USA.

Alice's artworks can be fun, thoughtful, touching – and angry. She has painted both small pieces and building-sized murals, all signed "Alice". The vast majority of Alice's work is of girls and women, featuring many full-face images.

"Alice Pasquini
is a multimedia
artist from Rome
whose affectionate
street art explores
the brighterside of
human relationships."

ALICEPASQUINI.COM

VHILS

Vhils is Alexandre Farto (1987–), and he was born in Lisbon, Portugal. He was decorating the urban landscape from a young age. Initially a graffiti artist, his art took a different turn after he studied art in London at Central Saint Martins.

Much of his work is sculpture, sometimes installations. He paints, creates from found objects, and carves images using tools, including electric drills and hammers. Vhils' work usually involves people (many of his works are faces), looking at how urban spaces change over time (his work is an active part of this), and themes of tradition, decay and progress.

"I have always been fascinated by how we are shaped by our places of origin, and subsequently by our surroundings."

VILS,
DONTTAKEFAKE.COM, 2023

"People say graffiti is ugly, irresponsible and childish. But that's only if it's done properly."

BANKSY,
WALL AND PIECE, 2005